Traditional MiniQuilts

by the Moon Over Mountain Quilters

Moon over MOUNTAIn
2 Public Avenue,
Montrose, PA 18801-1220
www.QuiltTownUSA.com

Moon Over Mountain
2 Public Avenue
Montrose, Pennsylvania 18801-1220

First Printing: 2006

Library of Congress Cataloging-in-Publication Data
Traditional miniquilts / by the Moon Over Mountain Quilters ; [compiled by Christiane Meunier].
     p.cm.
     ISBN 1—885588—68—2 (pbk.)
     1. Patchwork—Patterns. 2. Quilting.
     3. Miniature quilts. I. Meunier, Christiane.
     II. Moon Over Mountain Quilters.
     TT835.T726 2005
     746.46'041—dc22

                    2005015800

Design and Illustrations...........Diane Albeck-Grick
Photography.............................Van Zandbergen Photography,
                    Brackney, Pennsylvania

Our Mission Statement
We publish quality quilting books that recognize, promote, and inspire self-expression. We are dedicated to serving our customers with respect, kindness, and efficiency.

www.QuiltTownUSA.com

Introduction

What is your favorite part of quiltmaking? Is it the piecing or the quilting? Do you prefer sewing by hand or by machine? Whatever your favorite method, you'll be able to find a pattern in these pages that seems to call your name.

From the classic design of "Cait's Four Patch" and "Little Baskets", to the striking beauty of "Starring the Ladies" and "Bears in the Raspberries", the beautiful tradition of quilting is easy to keep alive when you make a miniature. Start with the tried-and-true methods you know or stretch yourself a bit and tackle a new quiltmaking technique. You'll find all the inspiration you need to get started with the flip of a page.

On the Cover

"Monkey Wrench Mania"
by Patricia Lacey
page 22

"Little Baskets"
by Jan Loschky
page 20

"Nine Patch and Diagonal Crosses"
by Constance Leavitt
page 4

Contents

6

16

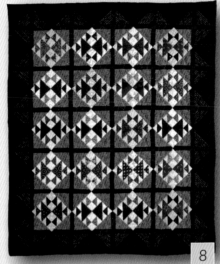

8

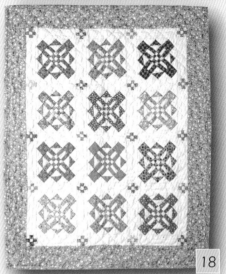

18

10

24

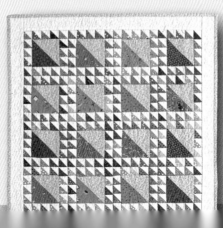

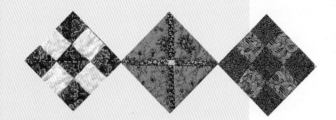

Constance Leavitt of Wichita, Kansas, hand pieced and hand quilted this miniature version of a *"Nine Patch and Diagonal Crosses"* wallhanging she saw in the Textile Museum in Lowell, Massachusetts. Constance enjoys using reproduction fabrics to replicate 18th and 19th century quilts.

Nine Patch and Diagonal Crosses

Quilt Size:
24 1/2" square

Block Size:
3" square

Materials
- Assorted print scraps
- 1/3 yard black
- 7/8 yard backing fabric
- 27" square of thin batting

Cutting

Dimensions include a 1/4" seam allowance.

For each of 24
Nine Patch blocks:
- Cut 5: 1 1/2" squares, one print
- Cut 4: 1 1/2" squares, contrasting print

For each of 25
Diagonal Cross blocks:
- Cut 4: 3/4" x 2 3/4" strips, one print
- Cut 1: 3/4" square, contrasting print
- Cut 1: 4 1/4" print square, then cut it in quarters diagonally to yield 4 triangles

Also:
- Cut approximately forty-five 1"-wide print strips of various lengths from 4" to 7", for the outer borders
- Cut 4: 1" x 24" strips, black
- Cut 4: 1 1/4" x 30" strips, black, for the binding

Directions

For the Nine Patch blocks:
1. Lay out five 1 1/2" print squares and 4 contrasting 1 1/2" print squares. Join them to make a Nine Patch block. Make 24.

For the Diagonal Cross blocks:
Trim the seam allowances to 1/8" after pressing.

1. Sew two print triangles to a 3/4" x 2 3/4" strip. Press the seam allowances toward the strip. Make 2.

2. Sew two 3/4" x 2 3/4" strips to a 3/4" square. Press the seam allowances toward the strips.

3. Join the triangle units and the pieced strip. Trim the block to 3 1/2" square. Make 25.

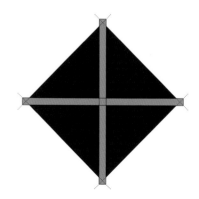

Assembly

1. Lay out the blocks alternately in 7 rows of 7. Sew the blocks into rows and join the rows.

2. Measure the length of the quilt. Trim two 1" x 24" black strips to that measurement. Sew them to opposite sides of the quilt.

3. Measure the width of the quilt, including the borders. Trim the remaining 1" x 24" black strips to that measurement. Sew them to the remaining sides of the quilt.

For the pieced borders:

1. Place two 1"-wide strips right sides together at a right angle. Sew the strips together, as shown. Continue adding strips to make a pieced strip at least 23" long. Make 2.

2. Lay the pieced strips beside opposite edges of the quilt.

3. In the same manner, make two strips each at least 24" long for the remaining sides, matching the prints on the ends with the ends of the first borders.

4. Trim the first pieced borders to fit and sew them to the quilt.

5. Trim the remaining borders to fit and sew them to the quilt.

6. Make 4 borders each at least 25" long and sew them to the quilt, as before.

7. Finish the quilt as described in the *General Directions*, using the 1 1/4" x 30" black strips for the binding.

Pam Abrams of Orlando, Florida, says that she is enamored with small scale piecing because it's a challenge. She practiced her skills on "Star Gazing," which includes a variety of designs in the centers of the stars. Pam has been a passionate quiltmaker for about 9 years.

Star Gazing

Quilt Size:
29 1/2" square

Block Size:
3" square

Materials

- Print scraps in various shades of light, medium, and dark in red, blue, tan, and green
- 1/4 yard blue print
- 1 yard red print
- 32" square of backing fabric
- 32" square of thin batting

Cutting

Dimensions include a 1/4" seam allowance.

For each of 5 Four Patch centers:
- Cut 2: 1 1/4" squares, light print
- Cut 2: 1 1/4" squares, dark print

For each of 3 Square-in-a-Square centers:
- Cut 1: 2" square, print
- Cut 4: 1 1/4" squares, contrasting print

For each of 3 Pinwheel centers:
- Cut 1: 1 5/8" square, light print
- Cut 1: 1 5/8" square, dark print

For each of 3 Star-in-a-Star centers:
- Cut 1: 1 1/4" square, print
- Cut 8: 7/8" squares, print
- Cut 4: 7/8" squares, contrasting print
- Cut 4: 7/8" x 1 1/4" rectangles, contrasting print

For each of 11 Variable Star centers:
- Cut 1: 2" square, print

For each of 25 Stars:
- Cut 4: 1 1/4" x 2" rectangles, light print
- Cut 4: 1 1/4" squares, same light print
- Cut 8: 1 1/4" squares, contrasting print

Also:
- Cut 4: 1" x 24" strips, blue print, for the inner border
- Cut 24: 3 1/2" squares, red print
- Cut 4: 4" x 30" strips, red print, for the outer border
- Cut 4: 1 1/4" x 40" strips, red print, for the binding

Directions

Trim the seam allowances to 1/8" after pressing.

For each Four Patch center:

1. Stitch a 1 1/4" light print square to a 1 1/4" dark print square. Make 2. Press the seams toward the dark.

2. Stitch the units together to make a Four Patch, as shown.

For each Square-in-a-Square center:

1. Draw a diagonal line from corner to corner on the wrong side of each 1 1/4" contrasting print square.

2. Place marked squares on opposite corners of a 2" print square. Stitch on the drawn lines. Press the squares toward the corners, aligning the edges. Trim the seam allowances to 1/8".

3. Place marked squares on the remaining corners. Stitch, press, and trim to complete a Square-in-a-Square.

For each Pinwheel center:

1. Draw a diagonal line from corner to corner on the wrong side of each 1 5/8" light print square.

2. Place a marked square on a 1 5/8" dark print square, right sides together. Stitch 1/4" away from the

drawn line on both sides, as shown. Make 2.

3. Cut the squares on the drawn lines to yield 4 pieced squares.

4. Lay out the squares in 2 rows of 2. Stitch the squares into rows and join the rows, as shown.

For each Star-in-a-Star center:

1. Place a 7/8" print square on one end of a 7/8" x 1 1/4" contrasting print rectangle. Stitch from corner to corner, as shown.

2. Press the square toward the corner, aligning the edges. Trim the seam allowance to 1/8".

3. Place a 7/8" print square on the opposite end of the rectangle. Stitch from corner to corner, as shown.

(continued on page 13)

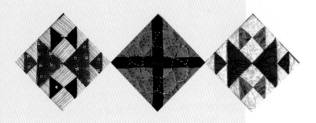

"Jan's Favorite" by Connie Chunn of Webster Groves, Missouri, is the result of a challenge to make a quilt using 2 different blocks. Connie used yellow and blue Double X blocks left over from another project, and added Devil's Puzzle blocks for the setting. She placed the fabrics strategically to give an illusion of borders. Connie named the finished quilt for her friend Jan, who exclaimed "That's my favorite!"

Jan's Favorite

Quilt Size:
18" x 21 3/4"

Block Size:
2 1/2" square

Materials

- 20 light print scraps each at least 7" x 8"
- 20 red print scraps each at least 4" square
- 20 blue print scraps each at least 2" x 4"
- Red solid at least 6" square
- 1/3 yard light brown
- 1/3 yard navy and red stripe
- 1/4 yard navy and red print
- 1/2 yard navy solid
- 20" x 24" piece of backing fabric
- 20" x 24" piece of thin batting

Cutting

Dimensions include a 1/4" seam allowance.

For each of 20 Double X blocks:

- Cut 1: 2 1/8" square, red print, then cut it in half diagonally to yield 2 triangles
- Cut 1: 1 1/2" square, same red print
- Cut 2: 1 1/2" squares, blue print
- Cut 5: 1 1/2" squares, light print, then cut 2 of them in half diagonally to yield 4 triangles
- Cut 4: 1 1/8" squares, same light print

For the Devil's Puzzle blocks:

- Cut 120: 7/8" x 2 3/4" strips, navy solid
- Cut 30: 7/8" squares, red solid
- Cut 20: 3 1/2" squares, light brown, then cut them in quarters diagonally to yield 80 triangles
- Cut 20: 2 1/2" squares, navy and red stripe, then cut them in half diagonally to yield 40 triangles

NOTE: *Cut these squares on the bias, as shown, to keep the stripes going in the right direction.*

Also:

- Cut 5: 4 7/8" squares, navy and red print, then cut them in quarters diagonally to yield 20 setting triangles. You will use 18.
- Cut 2: 2 3/4" squares, navy and red print, then cut them in half diagonally to yield 4 corner triangles
- Cut 3: 1 1/4" x 32" strips, navy solid, for the binding

Directions

For each Double X block:

1. Draw a diagonal line from corner to corner on the wrong side of each 1 1/2" light square.

2. Place a marked square on a 1 1/2" red square, right sides together. Stitch 1/4" away from the drawn line on both sides. Repeat with the remaining marked light squares and 1 1/2" blue print squares.

3. Cut the squares on the drawn lines to yield 6 pieced squares.

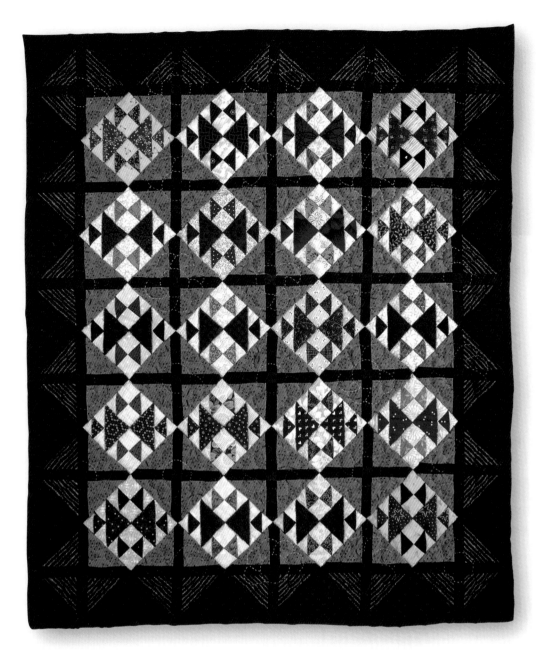

4. Lay out 2 blue pieced squares and two 1 1/8" light print squares. Join them as shown. Make 2.

5. Stitch 2 light print triangles to a red pieced square. Stitch the unit to a red triangle. Make 2.

6. Lay out the units and join them to make a block. Make 20.

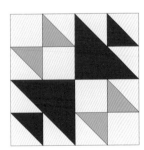

For the Devil's Puzzle blocks:

1. Stitch 2 light brown triangles to a 7/8" x 2 3/4" navy solid strip, as shown. Make 38.

2. Stitch a light brown triangle and a navy and red stripe triangle to a 7/8" x 2 3/4" navy solid strip, as shown. Make 4.

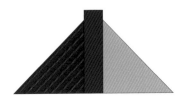

(continued on page 13)

Sara Madson of Crowley, Texas, designed "Bears in the Raspberries" so that her Teddy Bears could have their own quilt. Sara likes combining the soft lines of appliqué with the hard edges of patchwork. Her love of handwork is evident in the 1/4" diagonal quilting lines and the stippled border.

Bears in the Raspberries

Quilt Size:
28" square

Block Size:
5 1/4" square

Materials
- 1 yard muslin
- 1/2 yard red print
- 9 reproduction prints each at least 8" square, for the pieced blocks
- Fat quarter (18" x 20") dull green for the appliqué stems
- Green print at least 10" x 12" for the large leaves
- 2 green prints, each at least 12" square, for the small leaves
- Red scrap at least 8" square for the berries
- 30" square of backing fabric
- 30" square of thin batting

Cutting

Dimensions include a 1/4" seam allowance.
- Cut 4: 3 3/4" x 29" lengthwise strips, muslin
- Cut 2: 1 1/2" x 21" lengthwise strips, muslin
- Cut 2: 1 1/2" x 18" lengthwise strips, muslin
- Cut 2: 1 3/8" x 18" lengthwise strips, muslin
- Cut 6: 1 3/8" x 5 3/4" strips, muslin
- Cut 18: 3 1/2" squares, muslin
- Cut 36: 1 1/4" x 2 3/4" rectangles, muslin
- Cut 36: 1 1/4" squares, muslin
- Cut 4: 1 1/4" x 22" strips, red print
- Cut 1 1/4"-wide bias strips, red print, to equal at least 112" when joined for the binding

For each of 9 Bear's Paw blocks:
- Cut 2: 3 1/2" squares, print
- Cut 4: 2" squares, same print
- Cut 1: 1 1/4" square, same print

For the appliqué border:
The appliqué patterns (page 12) are full size and do not include a turn-under allowance. Make a template for each piece. Trace around the templates on the right side of the fabric and add a 1/8" to 3/16" turn-under allowance when cutting the fabric pieces out.
- Cut 1/2"-wide bias strips, dull green, to equal at least 175" for the stems
- Cut 28: large leaves, one green print
- Cut 128: small leaves, assorted green prints
- Cut 72: berries, red print

Directions

Trim seam allowances to 1/8" after pressing.

For each Bear's Paw block:
1. Draw diagonal lines from corner to corner on the wrong side of each 3 1/2" muslin square. Draw horizontal and vertical lines through the center.
2. Place a marked muslin square on a 3 1/2" print square, right sides together. Stitch 1/4" away from the diagonal lines on both sides. Make 2.

3. Cut on the drawn lines to yield 16 pieced squares. Trim each pieced square to 1 1/4" square.
4. Join 2 pieced squares and stitch the unit to a matching 2" print square.

5. Lay out 2 pieced squares and a 1 1/4" muslin square. Stitch them together. Make 4.

6. Stitch a unit to the first unit to make a paw. Make 4.

7. Lay out the 4 paws, a matching 1 1/4" print square, and four 1 1/4" x

2 3/4" muslin rectangles. Stitch them into rows and join the rows to make a Bear's Paw block. Make 9.

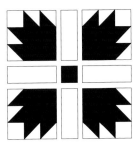

Assembly

1. Referring to the quilt photo, lay out the blocks with the 1 3/8" x 5 3/4"

muslin sashing strips between them in horizontal rows. Place the 1 3/8" x 18" muslin sashing strips between the rows.

2. Stitch the blocks and vertical sashing strips into rows. Join the rows and horizontal sashing strips.

3. Stitch the 1 1/2" x 18" muslin strips to the top and bottom.

4. Measure the length of the quilt. Trim the 1 1/2" x 21" muslin strips to that measurement. Stitch them to the sides of the quilt.

5. Measure the width of the quilt, including the borders. Trim 2 of the

1 1/4" x 22" red print strips to that measurement. Stitch them to the top and bottom of the quilt.

6. Measure the length of the quilt. Trim the remaining 1 1/4" x 22" red print strips to that measurement and stitch them to the sides of the quilt.

7. In the same manner, trim the 3 3/4" x 29" muslin strips to fit the quilt's width and stitch them to the top and bottom of the quilt.

8. Trim the remaining 3 3/4" x 29" muslin strips to fit the quilt's length and stitch them to the sides of the quilt.

For the appliquéd border:

1. Trace the border appliqué design on a piece of tracing paper. Place the quilt over the tracing paper and transfer the design lightly to the muslin border with a pencil or washout marker. Use a light box or a bright window to make the lines easier to see.

2. To appliqué the tiny stems, press a 1/2" dull green print bias strip in half lengthwise, right side out. Appliqué the folded edge along the drawn line of the stem. Carefully trim the underneath seam allowance to 1/8" after the strip is stitched. Because one side has already been stitched, the narrow stem fabric will be easier to handle. Tuck under and stitch the remaining side of the stem, making as narrow a stem as you can. The ends of the stems are covered by leaves or by the main stem.

3. Appliqué the large leaves over the ends of the stems.

4. Appliqué small leaves where indicated.

5. Appliqué the berries in groups of 3 along the stem.

6. Finish the quilt as described in the *General Directions*, using the 1 1/4"-wide red print bias strips for the binding.

(continued from page 7)

4. Press and trim as before to complete a star point unit. Make 4.

5. Lay out the star point units, the 1 1/4" print square, and four 7/8" contrasting print squares. Stitch them into rows and join the rows to make a star.

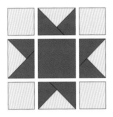

For each Variable Star Block:

1. Place a 1 1/4" print square on one end of a 1 1/4" x 2" contrasting print rectangle. Stitch from corner to corner, as before.

2. Press the square toward the corner, aligning the edges. Trim the seam allowance to 1/8".

3. Place a 1 1/4" print square on the opposite end of the rectangle. Stitch from corner to corner.

4. Press and trim to complete a star point unit. Make 4.

5. Lay out the star point units, the 2" print square, and four 1 1/4" light print squares. Stitch them into rows and join the rows to make a block. Make 11 using the 2" print squares for the centers.

6. Make 14 blocks in the same manner, using the pieced centers.

Assembly

1. Referring to the quilt photo on page 7, lay out the Star blocks and the 3 1/2" red print squares in 7 rows of 7.

2. Stitch the blocks and squares into rows. Join the rows.

3. Measure the length of the quilt. Trim two 1" x 24" blue print strips to that measurement. Stitch them to opposite sides of the quilt.

4. Measure the width of the quilt, including the borders. Trim the remaining 1" x 24" blue print strips to that measurement. Stitch them to the remaining sides of the quilt.

5. In the same manner, trim two 4" x 30" red print strips to fit the quilt's length and stitch them to the quilt.

6. Trim the remaining 4" x 30" red print strips to fit the quilt's width and stitch them to the quilt.

7. Finish the quilt according to the *General Directions*, using the 1 1/4" x 40" red print strips for the binding.

(continued from page 9)

3. Stitch 2 navy and red stripe triangles to a 7/8" x 2 3/4" navy solid strip in the same manner. Make 18.

4. Stitch two 7/8" x 2 3/4" navy solid strips to a 7/8" red solid square to make a center strip. Make 30.

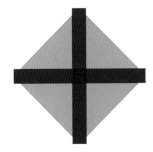

5. Stitch 2 light brown sections to a center strip, as shown. Make 12.

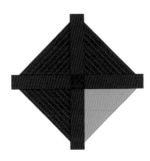

6. Stitch a light brown section and a navy and red stripe section to a center strip in the same manner. Make 14.

7. Stitch two of the remaining triangle sections to a center strip to make a corner block, as shown. Make 4.

8. Trim each Devil's Puzzle block to 3" square.

Assembly

1. Lay out the blocks and the setting and corner triangles in diagonal rows, as shown in the Assembly Diagram.

2. Stitch the blocks and triangles into rows and join the rows.

3. Finish the quilt as described in the *General Directions*, using the 1 1/4" x 32" navy solid strips for the binding.

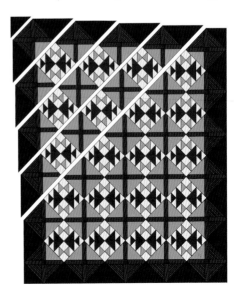

Gwen Hurlburt of Eugene, Oregon, was inspired by Sir Walter Scott's epic poem to make "**Lady of the Lake.**" This is just one of the many miniature quilts Gwen has made using 1930's reproduction prints.

Lady of the Lake

Quilt Size:
23" square

Block Size:
5" square

Materials

- Fat quarter (18" x 20") light blue print
- Assorted pink, blue, green, purple, and yellow prints, each at least 4" square
- 1/3 yard white
- 25" square of backing fabric
- 25" square of thin batting

Cutting

Dimensions include a 1/4" seam allowance.
- Cut 5: 1 1/4" x 20" strips, light blue print, for the binding
- Cut 8: 3 7/8" squares, light blue print
- Cut 8: 3 7/8" squares, assorted prints
- Cut 32: 3 3/4" squares, assorted prints
- Cut 4: 2" x 25" strips, white, for the border
- Cut 32: 3 3/4" squares, white

Directions

1. Draw a diagonal line from corner to corner on the wrong side of each 3 7/8" light blue print square.

2. Place a marked light blue square on a 3 7/8" print square, right sides together, Stitch 1/4" away from the drawn line on both sides, as shown. Make 8.

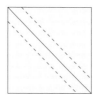

3. Cut the squares on the drawn lines to yield 16 large pieced squares. Press the seam allowances away from the light blue.

4. Draw diagonal lines from corner to corner on the wrong side of each 3 3/4" white square. Draw horizontal and vertical lines through the centers.

5. Place a marked white square on a 3 3/4" print square, right sides together. Stitch 1/4" away from both sides of the diagonal lines, as shown. Make 32.

6. Cut the squares on the drawn lines to yield 256 small pieced squares. Press the seam allowances toward the print.

7. Stitch 3 small pieced squares together, as shown. Make 32.

8. Stitch 5 small pieced squares together, as shown. Make 32.

9. Stitch two 3-square sections to opposite sides of a large pieced square, as shown.

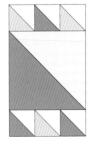

10. Stitch two 5-square sections to the remaining sides to complete the block. Make 16.

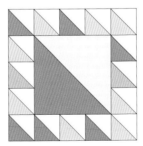

Assembly

1. Referring to the quilt photo, arrange the blocks in 4 rows of 4.

2. Stitch the blocks into rows and join the rows.

3. Measure the width of the quilt. Trim two 2" x 25" white strips to that measurement. Stitch them to opposite sides of the quilt.

4. Measure the length of the quilt, including the borders. Trim the remaining 2" x 25" white strips to that measurement. Stitch them to the remaining sides of the quilt.

5. Finish the quilt as described in the *General Directions*, using the 1 1/4" x 20" light blue print strips for the binding.

Toby Lischko of Robertsville, Missouri used Moda fabrics to make "Improved Nine Patch." This design's curves are clearly delineated by the contrast between the light and dark prints.

Improved Nine Patch

Quilt Size:
16 1/2" square

Block Size:
3 3/4" square

Materials
- 13 dark prints each at least 10" square
- 13 light prints each at least 10" square
- 19" square of backing fabric
- 19" square of batting

Cutting

The patterns (page 30) are full size and include a 1/4" seam allowance, as do all dimensions given.

For each of 9 dark blocks:
- Cut 4: 1 1/4" x 2 1/4" rectangles, one dark print
- Cut 4: B, same dark print
- Cut 4: 2 1/4" squares, one light print
- Cut 1: 1 1/4" square, same light print

For each of 4 light blocks:
- Cut 4: 1 1/4" x 2 1/4" rectangles, one light print
- Cut 4: B, same light print
- Cut 4: 2 1/4" squares, one dark print
- Cut 1: 1 1/4" square, same dark print

Also:
- Cut 8: C, assorted dark prints
- Cut 4: D, assorted dark prints
- Cut 20: B, assorted light prints (16 in matching pairs and 4 assorted)
- Cut 12: 1 1/4" x 6" strips, assorted dark prints, for the binding (one to match each C and D)

Directions

For each dark block:
1. Lay out the 1 1/4" x 2" dark print rectangles, 2" light print squares, and 1 1/4" light print square. Stitch them into rows and join the rows to make a Nine Patch.

2. Place template A on the Nine Patch and trace around it. Cut on the drawn lines.

3. Stitch a matching dark print B to each side of the trimmed unit to complete the block. Make 9.

For each light block:
1. Make a Nine Patch as before, using four 1 1/4" x 2" light print rectangles, four 2" dark print squares, and a 1 1/4" dark print square.

2. Using template A, trim the Nine Patch, as before. Stitch matching light print B's to the sides to complete the block. Make 4.

Assembly

1. Referring to the photo and the Assembly Diagram, lay out the blocks on point. Place the pairs of light B's along the sides and the 4 assorted light B's in the corners. Place the dark C's along the sides and the dark D's in the corners.

2. Stitch the pairs of light B's to their adjacent C's. Stitch the remaining light B's to the dark D's.

3. Stitch the blocks, C units, and D units into diagonal rows. Join the rows.

4. Measure the distance between the points of the blocks on the sides of the quilt. Add 1/2" to that measurement (for the seam allowances) and trim the eight 1 1/4" x 6" dark print binding strips that match the C's, to that length.

5. Add 1" to the measurement (for the seam allowances and miters) and trim the 4 remaining 1 1/4" x 6" dark print binding strips to that length.

6. Keeping the strips in order, stitch them together end to end, making a circle. Press the seam allowances open.

7. Press one edge of the binding circle 1/4" toward the wrong side.

8. Stitch the binding to the quilt, mitering the corners and matching the dark print strips to the C's and D's.

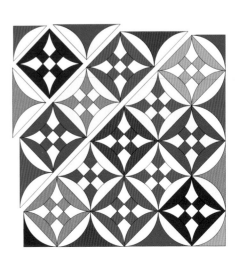

"Sonnie's Playhouse" was made from vintage and reproduction '30s scraps with a feedsack backing. Jayne Turner of Ottawa, Kansas, is often inspired by full size antique quilts to make her miniature ones.

Sonnie's Playhouse

Quilt Size:
16 1/4" x 20 1/2"

Block Size:
3 1/4" square

Materials
- Twelve 6" x 8" rectangles of assorted prints
- 1 yard muslin
- 1/4 yard pink print
- 19" x 23" piece of backing fabric
- 19" x 23" piece of thin batting

Cutting

Dimensions include a 1/4" seam allowance.

For each of 12 blocks:
- Cut 4: 1 1/4" squares, one print
- Cut 2: 1 5/8" squares, same print
- Cut 3: 3/4" x 8" strips, same print

Also:
- Cut 24: 1 5/8" squares, muslin
- Cut 36: 3/4" x 8" strips, muslin
- Cut 144: 1 1/4" squares, muslin
- Cut 31: 1 1/4" x 3 3/4" strips, muslin
- Cut 4: 2" x 18" strips, pink print, for the border
- Cut 2: 1 1/4" x 40" strips, pink print, for the binding

Directions

1. Draw a diagonal line from corner to corner on the wrong side of each 1 5/8" muslin square.

2. Lay a marked square on a 1 5/8" print square, right sides together. Stitch 1/4" away from the drawn line on both sides, as shown. Make 2 using the same print.

3. Cut the squares on the drawn lines to yield 4 pieced squares. Press the seam allowances toward the darker fabric.

4. Stitch a 3/4" x 8" muslin strip between two 3/4" x 8" print strips to make pieced strip A. Cut four 1 1/4" sections and three 3/4" sections from the pieced strip.

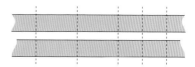

5. Stitch a 3/4" x 8" print strip between two 3/4" x 8" muslin strips to make pieced strip B.

6. Cut six 3/4" sections from the pieced strip.

7. Stitch a 3/4" section A between two 3/4" section B's to make a Nine Patch. Make 3. Set 2 aside.

8. Lay out the remaining Nine Patch, the pieced squares, 1 1/4" sections, the 1 1/4" print squares, and twelve 1 1/4" muslin squares, as shown.

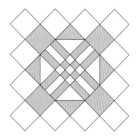

9. Stitch the squares into diagonal rows. Join the rows.

10. Center and trim the block to 3 3/4" square.

11. Repeat to make one block and 2 extra Nine Patches from each remaining print.

Assembly

1. Lay out the blocks, 20 Nine Patches, and the 1 1/4" x 3 3/4" muslin strips, as shown in the Assembly Diagram.

2. Stitch the Nine Patches and muslin strips into rows.

3. Stitch the muslin strips and blocks into rows. Join the rows.

4. Measure the length of the quilt. Trim 2 of the 2" x 18" pink print strips to that measurement and stitch them to the long sides of the quilt.

5. Measure the width of the quilt, including the borders. Trim the remaining 2" x 18" pink print strips to that measurement and stitch them to the short sides of the quilt.

6. Finish the quilt according to the *General Directions* using the 1 1/4" x 40" pink print strips for the binding.

Assembly Diagram

An antique doll quilt in *Miniature Quilts* magazine inspired Jan Loschky of Bartlett, Tennessee, to make *"Little Baskets."* She bought indigo woodblock prints and red reproductions especially for her project. Jan said she intentionally made her replica a little primitive like it might have been for a young girl's doll a long time ago.

Little Baskets

Quilt Size:
18 3/4" square

Block Size:
4" square

Materials
- 16 red and blue print scraps, each at least 5" square
- 8 shirting prints, each at least 8" square
- Fat quarter (18" x 20") blue print for the sashing
- 1/6 yard blue print for the binding
- 21" square of backing fabric
- 21" square of thin batting

Cutting

Pattern A is full size and includes a 1/4" seam allowance, as do all dimensions given.

From each red and blue print:
- Cut 1: A, print
- Cut 1: 3/4" x 4 1/4" bias strip, same print, for the handle
- Cut 1: 1 7/8" square, same print; then cut it in half diagonally to yield 2 small triangles

From each shirting print:
- Cut 1: 3 7/8" square, then cut it in half diagonally to yield 2 large triangles
- Cut 1: 2 7/8" square, then cut it in half diagonally to yield 2 small triangles
- Cut 4: 1 1/2" x 2 1/2" rectangles

Also:
- Cut 12: 1 1/4" x 4 1/2" strips, blue print, for the sashing
- Cut 3: 1 1/4" x 18 3/4" strips, blue print, for the sashing
- Cut 3: 1 1/4" x 30" strips, blue print, for the binding

Directions

1. Press a 3/4" x 4 1/4" bias strip in thirds, right side out. Trim 1/8" from each long edge.

2. Pin the pressed strip to a large shirting triangle and appliqué it in place, as shown.

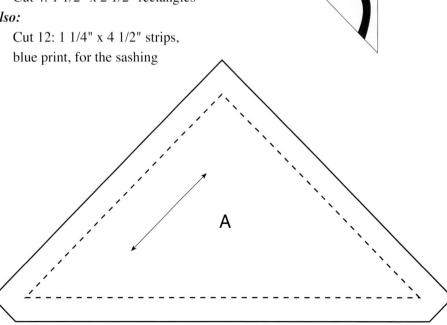

A

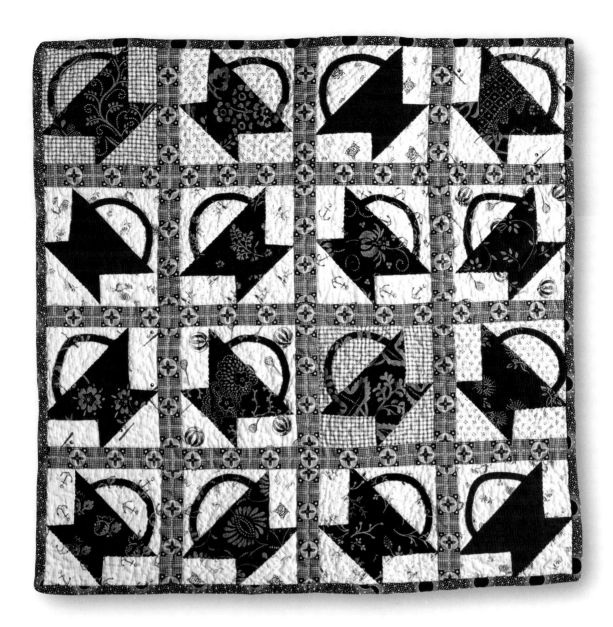

3. Stitch a print A to the appliquéd triangle.

4. Stitch a small print triangle to a 1 1/2" x 2 1/2" shirting rectangle. Stitch a matching small print triangle to a 1 1/2" x 2 1/2" shirting rectangle, reversing the direction of the triangle, as shown.

5. Stitch the units to the handle unit.

Stitch a small shirting triangle to the bottom to complete a Basket block. Make 16.

Assembly

1. Lay out the basket blocks, 1 1/4" x 4 1/2" blue print strips, and the 1 1/4" x 18 3/4" blue print strips. Stitch the blocks and 4 1/2" strips into rows.

2. Join the rows and 1 1/4" x 18 3/4" blue print strips.

3. Finish the quilt as described in the *General Directions*, using the 1 1/4" x 30" blue strips for the binding.

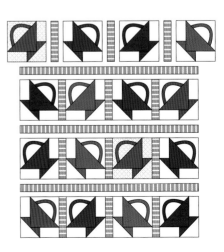

Patricia Lacey of Anaconda, Montana, used bits and pieces of her favorite fabrics to make 25 little blocks for "Monkey Wrench Mania." Her idea began as a sampler, but after making 6 blocks and deciding she really liked the Monkey Wrench, Patricia abandoned the first blocks. She used the orphan blocks on the back as a reminder that it's okay to change your mind.

Monkey Wrench Mania

Quilt Size:
29 1/4" square

Block Size:
3" square

Materials
- Assorted dark scraps
- Assorted light scraps
- 1/3 yard blue print for the sashing
- 1/4 yard gold print for the cornerstones
- 1/2 yard gold print for the outer border and binding
- 1/4 yard tan print for the setting triangles
- 1/4 yard cream for the inner border
- 1/6 yard blue for the piping
- 1 yard backing fabric
- 31" square of thin batting

Cutting

Dimensions include a 1/4" seam allowance.

For each of 25 blocks:
- Cut 1: 1 1/2" square, first print (center)
- Cut 2: 2" squares, second print
- Cut 2: 2" squares, light print (background)
- Cut 1: 1" x 6 1/4" strip, same light print (background)
- Cut 1: 1" x 6 1/4" strip, fourth print

Also:
- Cut 64: 1 1/4" x 3 1/2" strips, blue print, for the sashing
- Cut 40: 1 1/4" squares, gold print, for the cornerstones
- Cut 3: 6 5/8" squares, tan print, then cut them in quarters diagonally to yield 12 setting triangles
- Cut 2: 4 1/8" squares, tan print, then cut them in half diagonally to yield 4 corner triangles
- Cut 4: 1 1/2" x 26" strips, cream
- Cut 4: 1" x 31" strips, blue
- Cut 2: 3" x 31" strips, gold print
- Cut 2: 3" x 26" strips, gold print
- Cut 4: 1 1/4" x 34" strips, gold print, for the binding

Directions

1. Draw a diagonal line from corner to corner on the wrong side of each 2" background square. Place a marked square on a 2" second print square, right sides together. Sew 1/4" away from the drawn line on both sides. Make 2.

2. Cut the squares on the drawn lines to yield 4 pieced squares. Trim each pieced square to 1 1/2" square.

3. Sew the 1" x 6 1/4" background strip to the 1" x 6 1/4" fourth print strip along their length. Press the seam allowance toward the fourth print strip.

4. Cut four 1 1/2" sections from the pieced strip.

5. Lay out the pieced squares, 1 1/2" sections, and the 1 1/2" center square. Sew the units into rows and join the rows to complete the block. Make 25.

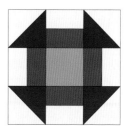

Assembly

1. Sew two 1 1/4" gold cornerstones to a 1 1/4" x 3 1/2" blue print strip. Make 2.

2. Sew 4 cornerstones and 3 strips together alternately. Make 2.

3. Sew 6 cornerstones and 5 strips together. Make 2.

4. Sew 8 cornerstones and 7 strips together. Make 2.

5. Lay out the blocks, remaining blue print strips, and pieced sashing strips according to the Assembly Diagram.

(continued on page 30)

"Starring the Ladies" definitely stands out in a crowd. This scrappy quilt looks at little intimidating, but with foundation piecing you'll be amazed at how quickly it goes together. Connie Chunn of Webster Groves, Missouri, designed this beautiful quilt using blocks from the Ladies Art Company.

Starring the Ladies

Quilt Size:

18" square

Materials

- Assorted red print scraps
- Assorted gold print scraps
- Beige print
- Assorted medium blue print scraps
- Assorted light prints for the stars
- Assorted dark blue print scraps
- Stripe at least 4" x 11" for a border
- 1/6 yard blue print for the outer border
- 1/6 yard navy for the binding
- 20" square of backing fabric
- 20" square of thin batting

Cutting

Fabric for foundation piecing will be cut as you piece the foundations. Refer to the General Directions, *as needed. All other dimensions include a 1/4" seam allowance.*

- Cut 1: 5" square, beige print, then cut it in quarters diagonally to yield 4 triangles
- Cut 4: 7/8" x 10 1/2" strips, stripe
- Cut 4: 7/8" squares, gold print
- Cut 4: 3 7/8" squares, assorted dark blue prints, then cut them in quarters diagonally to yield 16 large triangles. NOTE: *For more variety, cut extra squares then cut them into triangles. You will have some triangles left over to use in another project.*
- Cut 6: 2" squares, assorted dark blue prints, then cut them in half diagonally to yield 12 small triangles
- Cut 4: 3 7/8" squares, assorted red prints, then cut them in quarters diagonally to yield 16 large triangles NOTE: *Cut extras as described for the dark blue print triangles if desired.*
- Cut 10: 2" squares, assorted red prints, then cut them in half diagonally to yield 20 small triangles
- Cut 4: 5/8" x 16" strips, gold print

- Cut 4: 1 3/4" x 19" strips, blue print
- Cut 2: 1 1/4" x 40" strips, navy, for the binding

Directions

Follow the foundation-piecing instructions in the General Directions *to piece the foundations.*

1. Trace the full-size patterns (page 27) on foundation paper, transferring all lines and numbers. Cut each one out on the outer line. Make one Foundation A, 2 Foundation B, 4 each of Foundations C, D, E, F, G, H, and I, 24 each of Foundations J and K, 48 Foundation L, 48 Foundation M, and 96 of Foundation N.

2. Piece each foundation in numerical order using the following fabrics in these positions:

For Foundation A:
    1 - first dark red print
    2, 3 - beige print
For each Foundation B:
    1 - beige print
    2, 3 - first dark red print
For each Foundation C:
    1 - second dark red print
    2, 3, 4 - dark gold print
For each Foundation D:
    1, 3, 5, and 7 - beige print
    2, 4, and 6 - first dark red print

8 - light gold print

For each Foundation E:

   1, 3, 5, and 7 - beige print

   2, 4, 6, and 8 - first dark red print

   9 - light gold print

For each Foundation F and G:

   1 and 3 - first dark red print

   2 and 4 - beige print

   5 - second dark red print

For each Foundation H and I:

   1 and 3 - light print

   2 - first dark red print

   4 - second dark red print

   5 - beige print

For the Star blocks:

Piece one each of Foundations J and K and 2 Foundation L's for each Star block, using matching fabrics.

For each Foundation J:

   1 - medium blue print

   2, 3, and 4 - light print

For each Foundation K:

   1 - medium blue print

   2, 3 - light print

For each Foundation L:

   1 - medium blue print

   2, 3 - light print

   4, 5 - medium blue print

For the Double X blocks:

Piece 2 Foundations M's and 4 Foundation N's for each Double X block, using 2 red prints and one gold print.

For each Foundation M:

   1 - red print

   2, 3, 4 - gold print

   5 – same red print

For each Foundation N:

   1 - red print

   2, 3 - gold print

3. Trim the fabric 1/4" beyond the edges of each foundation.

For the Feathered Star:

1. Sew the Foundation B's to the Foundation A. Sew the Foundation

C's to the sides to complete the center of the Feathered Star.

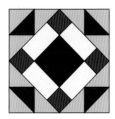

2. Sew a Foundation D to a beige print triangle, stitching only about 2/3 of the way, as shown.

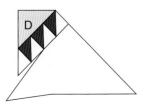

3. Sew a Foundation E to the triangle, stopping as before. Make 4.

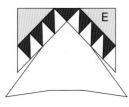

4. Sew a Foundation F to a Foundation H. Sew a Foundation G to a Foundation I. Make 4 of each.

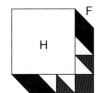

5. Sew 2 D/E units to opposite sides of the center unit.

6. Sew an F/H unit and a G/I to a D/E unit, keeping the triangle free. Complete the partial seams. Make 2.

7. Sew these units to the center unit then complete the partial seams.

For the Star block border:

1. Sew a Foundation J to a matching Foundation K. Sew 2 Foundation L's to the unit to make a Star block. Make 24.

2. Sew 5 Star blocks together to make a border. Make 2.

3. Sew the borders to opposite sides of the Feathered Star.

4. Sew 7 Star blocks together to make a border. Make 2. Sew them to the remaining sides of the Feathered Star.

For the Striped border:

1. Sew two 7/8" x 10 1/2" stripe strips to opposite sides of the quilt.

2. Sew the 7/8" gold print squares to the ends of the remaining 10 1/2"

strips. Sew the strips to the remaining sides of the quilt.

For the Double X blocks:

1. Sew 2 Foundation N's together to make an X unit, as shown. Make 2.

2. Join 2 Foundation M's and 2 X units to make a Double X block. Make 24.

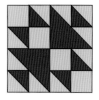

For the Double X border:

1. Choose 4 Double X blocks for the corners. Set them aside.

2. Lay out 5 Double X blocks, 4 large blue triangles, 2 small blue triangles, 4 large red triangles, and 2 small red triangles. Sew the blocks and triangles into diagonal rows and join the rows to make a border. Make 4.

3. Sew 2 borders to opposite sides of the quilt.

4. Place the remaining borders beside the quilt. Referring to the photo on page 25 for direction, place the reserved blocks in the corners and sew one small blue triangle and 3 small red triangles to each corner block.

5. Sew the corner blocks to the borders then sew the borders to the quilt.

Finishing

1. Measure the width of the quilt. Trim two 5/8" x 16" gold print strips to that measurement. Sew them to opposite sides of the quilt.

2. Measure the quilt in the opposite direction. Trim the remaining gold strips to that measurement. Sew them to the quilt.

3. In the same manner, measure the width of the quilt and trim two

1 3/4" x 19" blue print strips to that measurement. Sew them to opposite sides of the quilt.

4. Trim the remaining 1 3/4" x 19" blue print strips to fit and sew them to the quilt.

5. Finish the quilt as described in the *General Directions*, using the 1 1/4" x 40" navy strips for the binding.

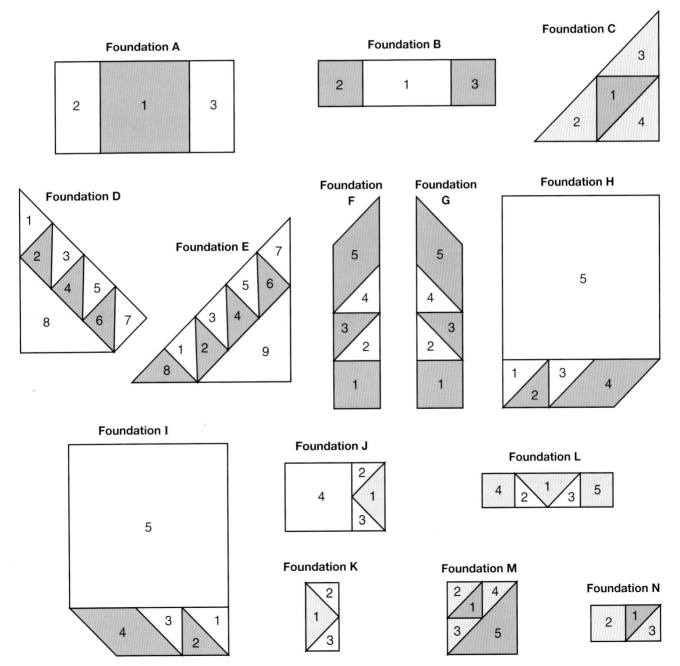

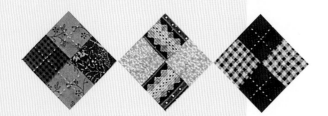

Debra Feece of Montrose, Pennsylvania, loves the scrappy look in her quilts. "Cait's Four Patch" looks perfect on her daughter Caitlin's antique doll bed.

Cait's Four Patch

Quilt Size:

21 1/2" square

Block Size:

2" square

Materials

- Assorted scraps of light, medium and dark prints, each at least 1 1/2" square
- Fat quarter (18" x 22") tan print
- 1/8 yard burgundy print
- 3/8 yard dark tan print
- 24" square of backing fabric
- 24" square of thin batting

Cutting

Dimensions include a 1/4" seam allowance. NOTE: *In this miniature, some of the blocks were pieced with 2 sets of matching squares, while in others each square is a different color. See "Make Them Match" for an easy way to stitch a Four Patch block with 2 sets of matching squares.*

- Cut 144: 1 1/2" squares, print scraps
- Cut 25: 2 1/2" squares, tan print
- Cut 5: 4 1/8" squares, tan print, then cut them in quarters diagonally to yield 20 setting triangles
- Cut 2: 2 3/8" squares, tan print, then cut them in half diagonally to yield 4 corner triangles
- Cut 4: 1" x 19" strips, burgundy print, for the inner border
- Cut 4: 2" x 22" strips, dark tan print, for the outer border
- Cut 3: 1 1/4" x 33" strips, dark tan print, for the binding

Directions

1. Stitch two 1 1/2" print squares together to make a pieced unit. Make 72.

2. Stitch 2 pieced units together to make a Four Patch. Make 36.

Assembly

1. Lay out the 36 Four Patches on point. Add the 2 1/2" squares, the setting triangles, and the corner triangles.

2. Stitch them into diagonal rows. Join the rows, as shown in the Assembly Diagram.

3. Measure the width of the quilt. Trim 2 of the 1" x 19" burgundy print strips to that measurement. Stitch them to opposite sides of the quilt.

4. Measure the length of the quilt, including the borders. Trim the remaining 1" x 19" burgundy print strips to

that measurement. Stitch them to the remaining sides of the quilt.

5. In the same manner, trim 2 of the 2" x 22" dark tan print strips to fit the quilt's width. Stitch them to opposite sides of the quilt.

6. Trim the remaining 2" x 22" dark tan print strips to fit the quilt's length and stitch them to the remaining sides of the quilt.

7. Finish the quilt according to *General Directions* using the 1 1/4" x 33" dark tan print strips for the binding.

Make Them Match

For an easy way to make "Cait's Four Patch" with 2 sets of matching squares per block, follow these cutting and stitching directions:

- Cut seventy-two 1 1/2" x 3 1/4" strips, print scraps

- Stitch 2 contrasting 1 1/2" x 3 1/4" strips, right sides together along their length, as shown. Make 36. ---------▶

- Press the seam allowance toward the darker fabric.

- Cut two 1 1/2" slices from each pieced strip. ----------------▶

- Stitch each pair of matching pieced strips together to make a Four Patch. ---------------------------------▶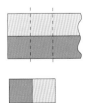

(continued from page 23)

6. Sew the blocks and the remaining 1 1/4" x 3 1/2" blue print strips into rows. Sew the pieced sashing strips to the appropriate block rows.

7. Sew the tan setting and corner triangles to the rows. Join the rows. Trim the edge 1/4" beyond the points of the outer cornerstones if necessary.

8. Measure the width of the quilt. Trim two 1 1/2" x 26" cream strips to that measurement. Sew them to opposite sides of the quilt.

9. Measure the length of the quilt, including the borders. Trim the remaining 1 1/2" x 26" cream strips to that measurement and sew them to the remaining sides of the quilt.

10. Trim the 3" x 26" gold strips to fit the quilt's width and sew them to opposite sides of the quilt.

11. Trim the 3" x 31" gold strips to fit the quilt's length and sew them to the remaining sides of the quilt.

12. Press the 1" x 31" blue strips in half right side out.

13. Measure the width of the quilt. Trim the pressed strips to that measurement.

14. Baste 2 strips to opposite sides of the quilt, aligning the raw edges. Baste the remaining pressed strips to the remaining sides in the same manner.

15. Finish the quilt as described in the *General Directions*, using the 1 1/4" x 34" gold print strips for the binding.

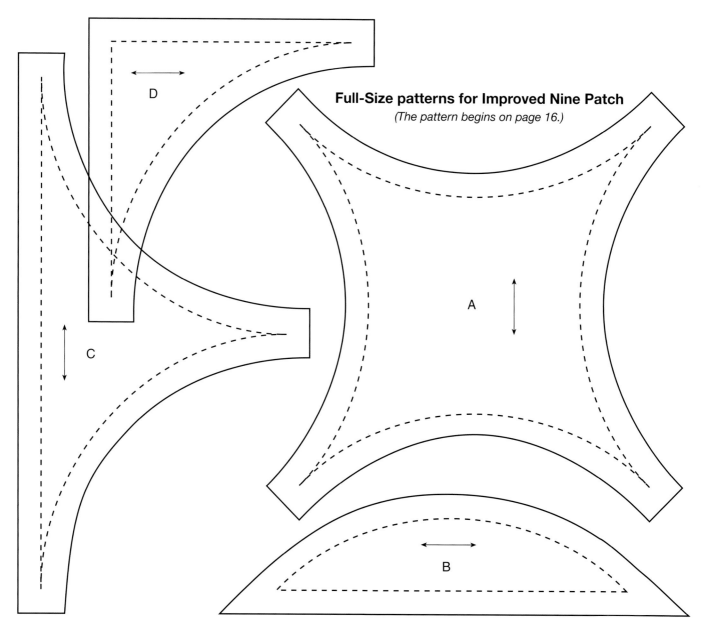

Full-Size patterns for Improved Nine Patch
(The pattern begins on page 16.)

General Directions

About the Patterns

Read through the pattern directions before cutting fabric for the quilt.

Fabrics

Yardage is based on fabric with a useable width of 40". We recommend using 100% cotton fabrics. We suggest washing your fabrics before using them.

Marking Fabric

Always test marking tools for removability. We suggest using silver or white marking tools for dark fabrics and fine-line pencils for light fabrics.

Templates

Template patterns are full size and, unless otherwise noted, include a 1/4" seam allowance. Trace patterns on clear plastic.

Pieced Patterns

For machine piecing, make templates with the seam allowance. Trace around the templates on the right side of the fabric. For hand piecing, make templates without the seam allowance. Trace templates on the wrong side of the fabric, flipping all directional (asymmetrical) templates before tracing, and add a 1/4" seam allowance as you cut the fabric pieces out.

Appliqué

Appliqué pieces can be stitched by hand or machine. To hand appliqué, baste or pin the pieces to the background in stitching order. Turn the edges under with your needle as you appliqué the pieces in place. Do not turn under or stitch edges that will be overlapped by other pieces. Finish the edges of fusible appliqué pieces with a blanket stitch made either by hand or machine.

To machine appliqué, baste pieces in place close to the edges. Then stitch over the basting with a short, wide satin stitch using a piece of tear-away stabilizer under the background fabric. You can also turn the edges of appliqué pieces under as for needleturn appliqué, and stitch them in place with a blind-hem stitch.

Foundation-Pieced Patterns

Place fabric pieces on the unmarked side of the foundation and stitch on the marked side. Center the first piece, right side up, over position 1 on the unmarked side of the foundation. Hold the foundation up to a light to make sure that the raw edges of the fabric extend at least 1/2" beyond the seamline on all sides. Hold this first piece in place with a small dab of glue or a pin, if desired. Place the fabric for position 2 on the first piece, right sides together. Turn the foundation over and sew on the line between 1 and 2, extending the stitching past the beginning and end of the line by a few stitches on both ends. Trim the seam allowance to 1/8". Fold the position 2 piece back, right side up, and press. Continue adding pieces to the foundation in the same manner until all positions are covered and the block is complete. Trim the fabric 1/4" beyond the edges of each foundation.

To avoid disturbing the stitches, do not remove the paper until the blocks have been stitched together and the borders have been added, unless instructed to remove them sooner in the pattern. The pieces will be perforated from the stitching and can be gently pulled free. Use tweezers to carefully remove small sections of the paper, if necessary.

Machine Sewing

Set the stitch length to 12 stitches per inch. Stitch pieces together from edge to edge unless directed to do otherwise in the pattern. When directions call for you to start or stop stitching 1/4" from the edges, as for set-in pieces, backstitch to secure the seam.

FINISHING
Marking Quilting Designs

Simple designs can be cut from adhesive-backed shelf paper. They'll stick and re-stick several times. Masking tape can be used to mark grids. Remove the tape when you're not quilting to avoid leaving

General Directions

a sticky residue. Mark lightly with pencils; thick lines that won't go away really stand out on a small quilt.

Batting

Use a thin batting. Layer the quilt sandwich as follows: backing, wrong side up, batting; quilt top, right side up. Baste or pin the layers together.

Quilting

Very small quilts can be lap-quilted without a hoop. Larger ones can be quilted in a hoop or small frame. Use a short, thin needle (between) and small stitches that will be in scale with the little quilt. Thread the needle with a single strand of thread and knot one end. Insert the needle through the quilt top and batting (not the backing) 1/2" away from where you want to begin quilting. Gently pull the thread to pop the knot through the top and bury it in the batting. Quilt as desired.

Binding

For most straight-edged quilts, a double-fold French binding is an attractive, durable and easy finish. NOTE: *If your quilt has curved or scalloped edges, binding strips must be cut on the bias of the fabric. Sew the binding strips together with diagonal seams; trim and press the seams open.*

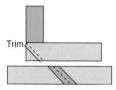

Trim one end of the strip at a 45° angle. Press one long edge of the binding strip 1/4" toward the wrong side. Starting with the trimmed end, position the binding strip, right sides together, on the quilt top, aligning the raw edge of the binding with the bottom edge of the quilt top. Leaving approximately 2" of the binding strip free, and beginning at least 3" from one corner, stitch the binding to the bottom of the quilt with a 1/4" seam allowance, measuring from the edge of the binding and quilt top.

When you reach a corner, stop the stitching line exactly 1/4" from the edge of the quilt top. Backstitch, clip threads, and remove the quilt from the machine. Fold the binding up and away, creating a 45° angle, as shown.

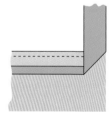

Fold the binding down as shown, and begin stitching at the edge.

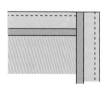

Continue stitching around the quilt to within 2" of the starting point. Lay the binding flat against the quilt, overlapping the beginning end. Open the pressed edge on each end and fold the end of the binding at a 45° angle against the angle on the beginning end of the binding. Finger press the fold.

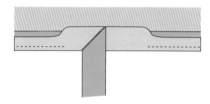

Trim 1/2" beyond the fold line. Place the ends of the binding right sides together and stitch with a 1/4" seam allowance. Finger press the seam allowance open.

Place the binding flat against the quilt and finish stitching it to the quilt. Trim the batting and backing even with the edge of the quilt top. Fold the binding over the edge of the quilt, and blindstitch the folded edge to back, covering the seamline.